THE SOURCE 12

Twelve Principles of Governance That Power Exceptional Boards

BoardSource®

PREAMBLE

Follow these 12 principles and advance the common good with uncommonly good work

Good governance is about providing critical capital — intellect, reputation, resources, and access — to power nonprofit success and thereby strengthen communities. It is more than checklists designed to detect and prevent problems, though boards must exercise their fiduciary duties with care. Good governance requires the board to balance its role as an oversight body with its role as a force supporting the organization.

Moving beyond the basics of governance, as important as those are, creates new opportunities. Exceptional boards add significant value to their organizations, making discernible differences in their advance on mission. Consider these examples: a board that drove higher performance through an emotionally powerful vision statement; a board that retained a talented executive in the face of high turnover among peers; a board that reshaped itself to meet the demands of a large fundraising campaign and exceeded its goals; and a board that had a waiting list for seats due to its reputation for having bright people doing consequential work. How does a board rise to this level? Are there standards that describe this height of performance?

BoardSource set about answering these questions. We convened a group of governance experts and, together, explored the characteristics of exceptional boards. Defining and analyzing their common traits and actions, we distilled the essence of what great boards do that is different and how they do it. The result — *The Source: Twelve Principles of Governance That Power Exceptional Boards*. These principles define governance not as dry, obligatory compliance, but as a creative and collaborative process that supports chief executives, engages board members, and furthers the causes they all serve.

To understand what made exceptional boards exceptional, we teased apart the difference between responsible and exceptional boards. Responsible boards are competent stewards. Focusing on fiduciary oversight, they ensure that their organizations comply with the law, act with financial integrity, and operate effectively and ethically. Exceptional boards add active engagement and independent decision making to this oversight function. Their members are open and honest with each other and the chief executive. They passionately challenge and support efforts in pursuit of the mission. The difference between responsible and exceptional boards lies in thoughtfulness and intentionality, action and engagement, knowledge and communication. This difference — the source of power — serves as the multiplier that powers exceptional boards.

Strong boards and strong chief executives make for good governance. Sharing a passion for serving their communities and constituents, they forge a dynamic relationship that leads to a higher level of performance. Exceptional boards, energized by a deep commitment to the work of their organizations, constantly search for solutions and seek to add value. Individual board members do substantive work that draws on their unique talents. Chief executives lead the organization adeptly, managing resources on a daily basis and regularly tapping into board talent.

The Source: Twelve Principles of Governance That Power Exceptional Boards enables nonprofit boards to operate at the highest and best use of their collective capacity. Aspirational in nature, these principles offer **chief executives** a description of an empowered board that is a strategic asset to be leveraged. They provide **board members** with a vision of what is possible and a way to add lasting value to the organizations they lead.

BoardSource 2005

ACKNOWLEDGEMENTS

This work reflects the collective wisdom of an extraordinary group of experts who have decades of experience researching, analyzing, counseling, advising, and serving on boards in both the nonprofit and for-profit sectors. We are deeply grateful for their insight and acumen in formulating these principles.

Nancy R. Axelrod
NonProfit Leadership Services

Marla J. Bobowick
BoardSource

Richard P. Chait
Harvard Graduate School of Education

Anne Cohn Donnelly
Kellogg School of Management, Northwestern University

Melissa Davis
YMCA of the USA

Deborah S. Hechinger
BoardSource

Richard L. Moyers
Eugene and Agnes E. Meyer Foundation

Roger W. Raber
The National Association of Corporate Directors

Celia Roady
Morgan, Lewis & Bockius, LLP

I

CONSTRUCTIVE PARTNERSHIP

Exceptional boards govern in constructive partnership with the chief executive, recognizing that the effectiveness of the board and chief executive are interdependent.

Nonprofit boards have primary legal responsibility for governance — the exercise and assignment of power and authority — of their organizations. Boards reserve to themselves organizational oversight and policy setting, and delegate to the chief executive responsibility for managing operations and resources. Exceptional boards are not just outside examiners, but also powerful forces supporting the organization and its chief executive.

While respecting this division of labor, exceptional boards become allies with the chief executive in pursuit of the mission. They understand that they and the chief executive bring essential, complementary ingredients to the governance partnership that, when combined, are greater than the sum of their parts. Exceptional boards recognize that they cannot govern well without the chief executive's collaboration and that the chief executive cannot lead the organization to its full potential without the board's unflagging support. Exceptional boards forge a partnership with the chief executive characterized by mutual trust, forthrightness, and a common commitment to mission. They encourage a strong, honest chief executive to pose questions and offer answers, and to share bad news early and openly. In turn, chief executives provide boards with tools and information to govern exceptionally. They welcome differing points of view and strategic thinking at the board table. Members of exceptional boards communicate regularly with the chief executive, informally discussing concerns in and between board meetings.

Exceptional boards hold the chief executive accountable. They evaluate the chief executive's performance annually and formally, and continually evaluate the organization's leadership needs as part of succession planning. As a sounding board and source of support, they encourage the chief executive to strengthen necessary skills. They understand that fair and competitive executive compensation is important in attracting and retaining qualified staff. When it is in the best interests of the organization, exceptional boards undertake the difficult task of replacing current leadership and selecting the most qualified chief executive available.

RESPONSIBLE BOARDS	THE SOURCE OF POWER	EXCEPTIONAL BOARDS
Delegate operations to chief executive	Trust, candor, and respect	Face and resolve problems early
Evaluate chief executive annually	Sharing good and bad news	Attract more qualified chief executives
Ensure fair and competitive compensation	Communication in and between meetings	Retain talented chief executives longer
Develop a job description with and for the chief executive	Open and honest chief executive	Change executive leadership at the right time
	Insightful tools and information	

MISSION DRIVEN ²

Exceptional boards shape and uphold the mission, articulate a compelling vision, and ensure the congruence between decisions and core values.

A nonprofit board's job starts with putting into words why the organization exists and what it hopes to accomplish. Exceptional boards, understanding their accountability to community and constituent needs, give voice to the enduring values, stories, and aspirations that shape the organization. They translate these elements into a compelling articulation of mission, vision, and core values that guides major decisions and everyday activities.

Exceptional boards treat questions of mission, vision, and core values not as exercises to be done once, but as statements of crucial importance to be drilled down and folded into deliberations. With the chief executive, exceptional boards develop, protect, and advance a clear mission that they use as a platform for advocacy, fundraising or grantmaking, and marketing.

To survive in a changing world, organizations must be focused and flexible. Exceptional boards take community and constituent needs into account when making decisions. They recognize when it is strategically essential for the organization to change course and, with the chief executive, help execute that transformation. As custodians of the mission, exceptional boards possess the boldness and courage to refocus the mission when permissible. In the best cases, the vision brings the mission to life. Alongside chief executives, exceptional boards develop a credible and persuasive vision of where the organization is going. Board and staff keep their eyes on this future prize. Both aspirational and inspirational, the vision provides a gripping call to action with overarching goals that motivate board and staff, and guide their decisions.

Exceptional boards make overt reference to institutional history. Recognizing that disagreements on strategy and policy are often rooted in conflicting values, exceptional boards seek to be explicit about the cultural norms that inform their behavior. With staff, they articulate core organizational values and translate them into action. Living those values, board members join the staff in serving as role models.

RESPONSIBLE BOARDS	THE SOURCE OF POWER	EXCEPTIONAL BOARDS
Articulate clear statement of mission	Use of mission, vision, and values in decision making	Sharply address community needs
Uphold organizational values	Congruence between mission, vision, values, and day-to-day work	Inspire staff to reframe strategies and elevate goals
	Willingness to refocus mission	Improve advocacy, fundraising, and marketing
		Maximize the value of grants and contributions

STRATEGIC THINKING ^{3}

Exceptional boards allocate time to what matters most and continuously
engage in strategic thinking to hone the organization's direction.

The essential role of a nonprofit board is to set organizational course; to provide direction; to look for horizons in years, not months. Exceptional boards do not relegate strategic thinking to a periodic exercise, but rather make it part of regular, ongoing board work. With guidance from management, they stay current with internal and external forces that drive change; they look backwards and forward to understand what has emerged and imagine what is possible. For these reasons, exceptional boards are able to explore the frameworks within which the organization operates and ask far-ranging questions that drive deeper, value-laden decisions.

In collaboration with the chief executive, exceptional boards allocate the lion's share of their time to issues of substantial consequence. Moving away from report-driven formats, agendas carve out time for meaningful discussion that shapes organizational strategy and actions. Meetings are well-attended in person, agendas feature only a few issues, and rich debate ensues. Working with senior staff, board members help clarify thorny problems, offer break-through insights on pressing issues, present new ways of framing challenges and opportunities, and actively generate important strategic ideas.

Strategic thinking derives from and drives strategic planning. Exceptional boards are active partners with staff in framing and assessing the strategic plan. Drawing on quantitative data and informed opinion and in concert with management, they affirm the organization's mission, chart a future course, and articulate priorities. As staff implements the strategic plan, the board monitors progress against financial and programmatic goals. Not only do they use strategic goals as a basis for assessing the chief executive and fine-tuning future plans, but they also use them to drive meeting agendas and shape board recruitment. Exceptional boards translate strategic priorities into action plans for themselves, identifying specific ways that the board and its members can contribute to the organization's success.

RESPONSIBLE BOARDS	THE SOURCE OF POWER	EXCEPTIONAL BOARDS
Set direction	Considerable time spent on consequential issues	Become a strategic asset and a source of leadership
Establish and review strategic plans	Constant strategic thinking	Sharpen direction, address difficult issues,
Monitor performance against plans	Joint board-staff efforts to frame and explore issues	identify opportunities
	Alignment of agendas and chief executive's goals with priorities	Generate solutions that are understood and supported

CULTURE OF INQUIRY ^{4}

Exceptional boards institutionalize a culture of inquiry, mutual respect, and constructive debate that leads to sound and shared decision making.

Responsibility for a nonprofit organization is vested in the board as a single corporate body, not in individual members. Success depends on attention to group dynamics. Exceptional boards, alongside their chief executives, create an environment based on respect and candor that fosters a productive exchange of views. They are not afraid to question each other or to challenge management.

Exceptional boards tackle their fiduciary duties efficiently to allow for robust and highly participative deliberations more often found at retreats. The chair energizes the group by skillfully managing the board's internal dynamics. Well-prepared with advance materials, board members respectfully listen to, acknowledge, and solicit different points of view. Exceptional boards not only raise questions from fiduciary and strategic perspectives, but also probe the frameworks within which decisions are proposed. Board members synthesize and aggregate diverse views to advance the dialogue. Exceptional boards seek more information, question assumptions, and challenge conclusions so that they may advocate for solutions based on analysis. Board members are able to voice their concerns before reaching a collective decision, which, once made, is supported by the entire board.

A culture that invites questions requires trust that is rooted in experience with fellow board members. Exceptional boards value personal relationships in a team setting and create opportunities for interactions among board and executive staff members. In conjunction with the chief executive, they develop and maintain processes that enable members to communicate among themselves and with staff and stakeholders, thereby broadening the board's sources of information and placing issues in context. Exceptional boards tap into the collective expertise of their members through appropriate group norms and processes. They recruit members who bring candor and reflection into the boardroom. They cultivate and distribute leadership across the board, rather than concentrating it in a handful of officers or an executive committee, so that the organization is not dependent upon particular individuals.

RESPONSIBLE BOARDS		THE SOURCE OF POWER		EXCEPTIONAL BOARDS
Have members who work well with each other		Mutual respect and trust		Engage and energize their members
Receive and review materials in advance		Actively-managed group dynamics		Expose full range of opinions
Convene well-organized meetings		Openness to questions, challenges, and differences of opinion		Make better decisions
Focus meetings on fiduciary duties		Multiple sources of information		Own and support their decisions

INDEPENDENT-MINDEDNESS ^{5}

Exceptional boards are independent-minded. When making decisions, board members put the interests of the organization above all else.

Board independence, a preeminent goal for corporate governance, is often narrowly defined by a list of tangible qualifiers. Compliance alone does not ensure good governance. More important is independent-mindedness, the ability to put the organization's interests first; to establish a point of view separate from that of the chief executive, staff, and board members; and to set aside personal agendas. By law, boards must adhere to the duty of loyalty, which requires that board members exercise their authority in the organization's best interests. Occasionally, situations occur in which board members have a duality of interests, reflecting allegiances to multiple entities. Exceptional nonprofit boards handle these situations through a conflict-of-interest policy that includes guidelines for disclosure, review, and recusal; have conflict-of-interest statements signed annually by board members and other individuals with decision-making power; and rigorously adhere to these procedures. Private foundation boards go even further to assure compliance with self-dealing prohibitions.

Exceptional boards recognize that independence depends as much on a frame of mind as on a set of circumstances. Their members do not allow their votes to be unduly influenced by loyalty to the chief executive or by seniority, position, or reputation of fellow board members, staff, or donors. Instead, they rely on thorough deliberation to uncover all facets of an issue and then distill their peers' perspectives into an autonomous and educated opinion.

To build a collective culture of independence, exceptional boards establish policies, processes, and norms that reinforce independent decision making. In collaboration with the chief executive, they interact purposefully with staff and outside stakeholders to gather information in pursuit of objectivity. During recruitment, exceptional boards avoid board members who have intrinsic conflicts of interest that cannot be managed. They encourage open debate that focuses on what is best for the organization, relying on their members' collective wisdom.

RESPONSIBLE BOARDS	THE SOURCE OF POWER	EXCEPTIONAL BOARDS
Adopt conflict-of-interest policies	Unqualified loyalty	Make decisions in the best interest of organization
Disclose and do not vote on matters of personal interest	Independent thinking drawn from multiple sources	Minimize risk of poor decisions and negative publicity
	Decision making free of undue influence	
	Rigorous conflict-of-interest procedures	

6

ETHOS OF TRANSPARENCY

Exceptional boards promote an ethos of transparency by ensuring that donors, stakeholders, and interested members of the public have access to appropriate and accurate information regarding finances, operations, and results.

Charitable status creates a special obligation to the organization's beneficiaries and the public for a nonprofit board. Government regulators, watchdog agencies, and the media play an active role in shaping public perception. Exceptional boards ensure the public has access to clear, accurate, and timely information that enables it to determine whether the organization is using its tax-exempt status appropriately. They make sure that the organization posts its IRS Form 990 or 990-PF on the organization's Web site and offers unencumbered access to audited financial statements and reports of programmatic accomplishments.

Exceptional boards understand that it is in the organization's best interests to develop open relationships with staff and donors, as well as stakeholders and the larger community. Working with staff, exceptional boards ensure that donors are treated with respect, receive forthright reports on use of their funds, and are apprised of notable developments. At the same time, they distinguish between the need for transparency and the importance of confidentiality. They ensure that policies and procedures protect the organization's competitiveness and the reputation of individuals affiliated with it.

Exceptional boards ensure that transparency is extended internally. They receive information of significance, and every board member has equal access to relevant materials when making decisions. Exceptional boards and their chief executives foster open exchange between board and staff members without undermining the critical relationship between the board and chief executive. They institute policies to ensure that staff will feel comfortable bringing appropriate matters to their attention. They also consider how transparency should inform board activities and to what extent governance practices should be made public.

RESPONSIBLE BOARDS		THE SOURCE OF POWER		EXCEPTIONAL BOARDS
Comply with government filing requirements		Active exchange between board and staff		Alongside staff, feel connected to the organization
Report annually on accomplishments and use of funds		Openness with donors and the public		Cultivate relationships with donors and stakeholders
		Whistle-blower policies to protect staff		Earn public trust and support

COMPLIANCE WITH INTEGRITY ⁷

Exceptional boards promote strong ethical values and disciplined compliance by establishing appropriate mechanisms for active oversight.

A board's fundamental task is to ensure that the organization operates legally and ethically. Ethics and compliance exist in a deep-seated partnership, reinforcing each other. Ethics elevates compliance to a noble purpose, and compliance grounds ethics in the practical realities of day-to-day work. Creating an organization that encourages exemplary conduct is the most effective way of preventing misconduct. Exceptional boards make certain that an explicit set of ethical values and standards have been candidly discussed, established, and clearly communicated to stakeholders of the organization.

Exceptional boards make vigorous oversight the norm. They ensure that internal controls and oversight mechanisms are established and implemented by management. Enough board members are financially literate and astute so that, collectively, the board can assess the organization's fiscal health. They expect the chief executive or chief financial officer to sign the IRS Form 990 or 990-PF, thereby taking responsibility for annual financial statements and attesting to their accuracy. They use oversight mechanisms, such as an independent audit, to ensure accountability and sufficient controls; to deepen their understanding of the organization; and to reduce the risk of waste, fraud, and abuse.

Exceptional boards recognize that certain oversight functions, such as executive compensation and audit, must report directly to the board. Recognizing that executive and board compensation are areas fraught with conflict and the potential for abuse, board members gather industry data or work directly with compensation consultants to review compensation proposals. They consider whether to establish a separate audit committee and whether the internal audit function should report directly to the board or the audit committee. To protect the organization's assets, exceptional boards also ensure that the organization has adequate insurance and contingency plans. Periodically, they ask management to review and report on current or potential risks to the organization. For their part, exceptional boards vigorously implement conflict-of-interest policies.

RESPONSIBLE BOARDS		THE SOURCE OF POWER		EXCEPTIONAL BOARDS

RESPONSIBLE BOARDS	THE SOURCE OF POWER	EXCEPTIONAL BOARDS
Ensure compliance with the law	Financially attentive and astute board members	Judiciously allocate and oversee resources
Approve budget and review financial reports	Vigorous oversight	Deeply understand their organizations
Obtain independent review or audit of financial statements	Proactive risk management	Minimize risk
Ensure appropriate insurance	Auditors and compensation consultants report to board	Display highest standards of ethical conduct
Revise bylaws, as necessary		

SUSTAINING RESOURCES

8

Exceptional boards link bold visions and ambitious plans to financial support, expertise, and networks of influence.

With the ultimate goal of delivering on the mission, boards must understand their non-profit's fiscal health. Exceptional boards, in collaboration with the chief executive, ensure that the organization has a clear financial plan that is aligned with strategic, operating, and development or philanthropic grant-making plans. Linking budgeting to strategic planning, they approve activities that can be realistically financed with existing or attainable resources. Within a larger frame of reference for resource generation, exceptional boards work closely with chief executives to diversify and maximize sustainable revenue sources so that the organization can achieve its goals. They engage with management to develop and monitor a portfolio of income streams, which may range from fundraising and sponsorship to earned income and for-profit subsidiaries to program-related and market investments.

Exceptional boards leverage a variety of intangible resources on behalf of the organization. They work with the chief executive to ensure that the organization has the infrastructure and internal capacity it needs, such as highly qualified employees, capable volunteers, adequate technology, and appropriate facilities.

Boards are responsible for approving budgets and contributing to their success. If fundraising is necessary, exceptional boards establish clear expectations for member participation in development activities and individual giving. Members of exceptional boards not only make personally meaningful contributions but also stretch further for special campaigns. They extend the reach of the organization by actively using their own reputations and networks to secure funds, expertise, and access. Members of exceptional boards bring intellectual power, as well as social and political capital, to the organization, thereby enhancing its reputation and capacity. They use their personal and business relationships to expand awareness of the organization and actively participate in cultivating partnerships and collaborations. Serving as the community face of the organization, they advocate on behalf of the organization in appropriate public contexts.

RESPONSIBLE BOARDS	THE SOURCE OF POWER	EXCEPTIONAL BOARDS
Approve balanced budget	Creative and diverse revenue sources	Generate increased revenue
Accept fundraising responsibilities and contribute personally	Enthusiasm for bold visions and ambitious plans	Extend programmatic capacity of organization
Develop and monitor investments	Active involvement in solicitations	Improve organization's standing in the community
Promote organization in community	Intellectual, social, political, and reputation capital	

RESULTS-ORIENTED ^{9}

Exceptional boards are results-oriented. They measure the organization's advancement towards mission and evaluate the performance of major programs and services.

In the absence of clear market mechanisms to provide feedback on the value and quality of programs, many boards monitor organizational performance by reviewing year-end reports of financial performance and programmatic progress; some use the audit committee to carry out this function. Exceptional boards take on the more difficult task of measuring overall efficiency, effectiveness, and impact. Boards and management must agree on critical indicators that flow from the organization's mission, vision, and strategic priorities and take into consideration community needs, comparable organizations, and the operating environment. To better monitor progress on a routine basis, exceptional boards invest in the thoughtful development of key indicators and in the organizational infrastructure to report on them.

Exceptional boards rigorously review the organization's performance, overall efficiency, and ultimate impact using a variety of measures. They draw on their own experiences, external feedback, and long-term financial metrics to monitor progress towards accomplishment of strategic plans. They also assess the quality of service delivery, integrate benchmarks against peers, and calculate return on investment. While staff gather and analyze data, exceptional nonprofit boards and chief executives share responsibility for monitoring and synthesizing this information. They use this information to make mid-course corrections, changing and refreshing strategic and operating plans as appropriate. They bring different, equally valuable perspectives to organizational assessment.

Monitoring progress against goals, however, can be limited by hindsight. Attentive to results, exceptional boards also use performance evaluation to ensure that their organizations are flexible and adaptable to changes in the environment. In close collaboration with staff, they use indicators to identify early successes so that they can maximize them, and potential problems in time to address them before they escalate. In thinking purposefully about the future, exceptional boards also consider the introduction, continuation, and cessation of new and existing programs.

RESPONSIBLE BOARDS		THE SOURCE OF POWER		EXCEPTIONAL BOARDS
Monitor financial performance		Incisive program evaluation		Maximize resource utilization without micromanaging
Receive programmatic updates		Meaningful performance metrics		Focus on outcomes, not inputs
		Early issue identification		
		Benchmarking against peers		Drive programmatic activities to excellence

INTENTIONAL BOARD PRACTICES

10

Exceptional boards intentionally structure themselves to fulfill essential governance duties and to support organizational priorities.

Drawing on bylaws, policies, and tradition, boards create structures and practices that guide how they come together as a governing body. While every board should determine how best to organize itself to carry out its duties, exceptional boards take ownership of their operations. They think explicitly about size, structure, and schedule of board operations. Particularly attentive to design and execution, they value efficiency and flexibility in leadership structures.

Making governance intentional, not incidental, exceptional boards connect their operations with the organization's unique circumstances. They study strategic priorities, institutional turning points, and leadership. To ensure that governance practices are up-to-date, they track emerging trends and adjust internal policies as appropriate. To provide stable leadership to the organization, they invest in structures and practices that transcend individuals, document them for institutional memory, and thoughtfully adapt them to changing circumstances. Deliberate about their own affairs, exceptional boards determine and adjust the optimal board size by assessing their responsibilities and organizational needs. When necessary, they establish permanent board committees, focusing especially on the financial and ethical integrity of the organization. They rely on ad hoc work groups to move forward on critical issues and take advantage of individual member's capabilities. They form executive committees when they improve the quality of governance, and they assign them clearly defined roles.

Exceptional boards make meetings matter. They translate challenges and opportunities into board agendas that allow them to make meaningful decisions in a timely manner. They improve meeting efficiency by relying on consent agendas. They often meet in executive sessions with and without the presence of the chief executive — not to escape difficult decisions, but to allow for confidential discussion. They keep accurate meeting minutes that record actions taken for posterity and to protect board members and the organization.

RESPONSIBLE BOARDS		THE SOURCE OF POWER		EXCEPTIONAL BOARDS
Design board size, structures, and meetings to accomplish work of the board		Intentional and strategic approach to board operations		Engage in action-oriented, results-driven work
Document practices, policies, and decisions		Flexibility in response to changing environment		Use board member time wisely
		Member assignments aligned with priorities		Reap full benefit of members' talents
		Executive sessions		Connect to the work of the organization

CONTINUOUS LEARNING

Exceptional boards embrace the qualities of a continuous learning organization, evaluating their own performance and assessing the value they add to the organization.

onprofit board work does not always come naturally to members. Motivated by a passion for the organization's cause, they need guidance in governance duties, nonprofit practices, and the field of their organization's endeavor. Exceptional boards not only ensure that all members participate in a formal orientation and continuous education, but also use orientation as a way to enhance board relationships, traditions, and teamwork.

The professional expertise and personal experience that board members bring from their individual lives is important but not sufficient for effective governance. Through ongoing board education, exceptional boards deepen members' knowledge about their organization's industry, peers, larger societal trends, and other environmental factors. They embed learning opportunities into routine governance work and cultivate them outside of the boardroom. They systematically and collectively reflect on critical incidents in the organization's history — identifying and learning from experiences — and tap into a wide range of past, present, and future stakeholders.

With openness to reflection and continuous improvement, exceptional boards gather feedback on their collective productivity and unique contribution to the organization. They undertake periodic board assessments to evaluate their own performance and thereby strengthen board structures and practices. They use a combination of routine and periodic evaluations to improve meetings, restructure committees, and address individual member performance. They rely on situational assessments during extraordinary events when the board must be able to respond properly to challenges.

Exceptional boards invest time and resources in board development. Over time, board members deepen their commitment to the organization, making them increasingly valuable to its success. The board functions well collectively and in collaboration with senior management. The organization, in turn, is able to maximize the unique and collective judgment, wisdom, and thoughtfulness of the board in pursuit of its mission and vision.

RESPONSIBLE BOARDS		THE SOURCE OF POWER		EXCEPTIONAL BOARDS
Orient new board members		Learning activities built into board work		Are well-informed about the external environment
Use board members' skills		Knowledge drawn from outside the boardroom		Grow on the job, and contribute at increasing levels
		Board evaluation of individual and collective performance		Regularly upgrade their governance practices

REVITALIZATION

12

Exceptional boards energize themselves through planned turnover, thoughtful recruitment, and inclusiveness.

Board composition is critical to success. A nonprofit board represents a pool of talent into which the organization can tap to further its mission. Many boards revitalize themselves through term limits and a well-defined process for recruitment that assesses future organizational needs and current board member competencies. Exceptional boards see the correlation between mission, strategy, and board composition. They recognize that diversity and inclusiveness are essential to organizational success. They seek diversity in terms of personal and professional backgrounds and experiences, and they welcome differing voices and an array of perspectives. They are acutely aware of the need for members who possess knowledge of the nonprofit sector, superior financial acumen, ability to secure funding, and personal characteristics and experiences that positively enrich group interaction. They also use board composition as a strategy to increase understanding of their constituencies and community needs.

Exceptional boards delegate recruitment, orientation, and ongoing education to a committee whose purview extends beyond nominations to board development. Along with the chief executive, they recruit candidates to strengthen board capacity in terms of expertise and group dynamics. Recruitment is continuous, with individual members sharing responsibility for identifying and cultivating new candidates. They consciously and conscientiously inform candidates and new members of their responsibilities and expectations. Recognizing the importance of board leadership development and succession planning, they groom chairs and officers purposefully through a transparent and participatory process.

Exceptional boards understand the importance of fresh perspectives and the risks of closed groups. They rigorously evaluate board member participation before extending terms and often use term limits to rejuvenate themselves. They remove ineffective members to maintain a sense of shared responsibility among the board. They find creative alternatives to keep valuable members associated with the organization after their terms expire.

RESPONSIBLE BOARDS		THE SOURCE OF POWER		EXCEPTIONAL BOARDS
Recruit based on individual competencies and personal connections		Clarity around expectations of board members		Know their roles and function well as a group
Establish a committee to manage the recruitment process		Diversity of perspectives		Include important voices at the board table
		Continuous recruitment		Have a ready supply of new board members
		Thoughtful use of term renewals		Experience smooth leadership transitions
		Officer succession planning		

BLUE RIBBON PANEL

The following individuals provided invaluable guidance, comments, and insights in reviewing *The Source: Twelve Principles of Governance That Power Exceptional Boards*. We are deeply grateful to each of them for their willingness to contribute their time, talent, experiences, and wisdom to this effort.